BEAUTIFUL HAIR

BOOK, LYRICS & MUSIC BY RONVÉ O'DANIEL

MUSIC BY JEVARES MYRICK

Uproar Theatrics

LICENSING & PRODUCTION INQUIRIES
Uproar Theatrics, LLC.
hello@uproartheatrics.com I www.UproarTheatrics.com

Beautiful Hair
Book and Lyrics copyright © 2021 by Ronvé O'Daniel
Music copyright © 2021 by Ronvé O'Daniel & Jevares Myrick

Beautiful Hair is published by Uproar Theatrics, LLC
500 8th Ave FRNT 3, #1714 New York, NY 10018

ISBN: 978-1-968051-06-8

First Printing, May 2025

CAST OF CHARACTERS

JAMILA, an African American Girl/Woman, late teens/mid 20's. Quirky, charming, intelligent and wise beyond her years. Michelle Obama is totally her spirit animal and she wants nothing more than to attend Princeton just like her. Think Lyric Ross with a little bit of Willow Smith with the vocal range of Chloe x Halle. Strong singer/actress, rap and dance is a plus. Soprano with a pop belt.

HARPER, an African American Girl/Woman, late teens/mid 20's. The antagonist and most popular girl in school (duh), attractive, confident and energetic. She's someone who is never told "no"...she always gets what she wants, when she wants it - otherwise, there's trouble! Strong rapper/dancer/singer/actress. Yara Shahidi with the confidence of a Meg Thee Stallion. Pop soprano.

MARCUS, an African American Boy/Man, late teens/ mid 20's. Charming, funny/comedic, handsome, undeniable swagger...and completely oblivious to it all - but he's lovable despite that. Strong rapper/singer/ actor who moves well. A young Damon Wayans Jr. With a dash of Lamorne Morris mixed with the talent of an Usher.

NYEMA, an African American Woman mid/late 20s, part of Ensemble. Jamila's older sister and #1 supporter. Fun, blunt, single and always looking to mingle, comedic - the right balance of righteous and ratchet, but most importantly: she's unapologetic about who she is and where she comes from. Keke Palmer with a flair of Amanda Seales. Alto with a strong belt.

INTERVIEWER 1, a Woman, Man, or Gender Fluid/ Non-binary, any ethnicity, late 20s, early 30s. The person most responsible for single-handedly making Jamila's life more complicated than it already is! Must be a strong rapper/actor/actress. Alto/baritone.

INTERVIEWER 2, a Woman, Man, or Gender Fluid/ Non-binary, any ethnicity, early-mid 30s. A friendly, mentor-type who only wants to see the best out of Jamila. Could be a guest-star cameo. Actor.

ENSEMBLE, All types, all ethnicities late teens/early 20s with the ability to portray students, civilians, friends and bullies. Must be strong singers/actors/ dancers.

PRODUCTION NOTES

Jamila must wear knotless braids, specifically. As opposed to any other hair style exclusive to black girls/women. Knotless braids is a specific hairstyle that will reveal its significance in the show.

MUSICAL NUMBERS

1. Beautiful Hair Overture

2. Undeniable *(Jamila, Nyema, Ensemble)*

3. Class In Session *(Harper, Jamila, Ensemble)*

4. Like A Sister *(Marcus, Jamila)*

5. The Interview *(Harper, Jamila, Interviewer, Ensemble)*

6. What Would Michelle Do? *(Marcus, Jamila, Ensemble)*

7. Your Roots *(Nyema, Jamila)*

8. One of One: Finale *(Jamila, Company)*

ACKNOWLEDGEMENTS/ THANK YOU

City Springs Theatre Company - Sandy Springs, GA
Kayce Grogan-Wallace
Amber Iman
Jasmin Richardson
Stephanie Leah Evans

<u>SCENE 1: JAMILA'S HOME, PRESENT DAY</u>

<u>SONG: "OVERTURE"</u>

> *(Lights up on JAMILA and NYEMA in their living room. JAMILA sits in a chair, staring forward at a mirror. JAMILA'S hair has been washed, conditioned, blown out and straightened. NYEMA stares at JAMILA'S hair still deciding what style she wants to do.)*

NYEMA
Jamila, Jamila. My little sister's growing up. Getting ready for college interviews!

JAMILA
Alright Nyema: I need you to come correct on my hair today. This is important.

NYEMA
Listen, North State Technical College ain't ready for the engineering job I'm about to perform on this head of yours.

JAMILA
That's what I like to hear!

NYEMA
So what we doin'? Beyonce *Lemonade*? Lupita Bantu *Black Panther* look? Or I can wig you up and give you that Michelle Obama? This could be your practice for Princeton!

JAMILA
You know Michelle is my girl, but I don't do wigs.

NYEMA

Of course I know. You haven't put her book down since I
bought it for you!

JAMILA

She speaks to me.

NYEMA

Let's hope she's speaks to you about this interview.

JAMILA

I can't believe it's tomorrow. It crept up fast!

NYEMA

It sure did. And Princeton will creep up just as fast.

JAMILA

I can't even think about Princeton yet.

NYEMA

You better start. Mom works too hard for you to entertain
that idea. It's on you now sis.

JAMILA

That's a lot of pressure for a school with a five point eight
acceptance rate.

NYEMA

That's why you gotta claim it! Jamila Watkins: Valedictorian.
Princeton graduate!

JAMILA

Can you imagine?

NYEMA

You'd be set for life. That's why we gotta get you right.
Can't have you out here lookin' crazy.

SONG: "UNDENIABLE"

NYEMA

BEAUTIFUL HAIR.
IT STARTS WITH BEAUTIFUL HAIR.

NYEMA/JAMILA

BEAUTIFUL HAIR.
IT STARTS WITH BEAUTIFUL HAIR.

JAMILA

FIRST IMPRESSIONS ARE THE MOMENTS THAT
AFFECT YOUR
FUTURE AS A GROWN
ADULT WHO YEARNS TO LIVE THEIR DREAM
CAREER AND
MOVE UP ON THEIR OWN.
I HAVE TO WOW THEM FOR MY DESIRED
OUTCOME
AND THERE SHOULD BE DOUBT WHEN YOU
MEASURE
MY IMPRESSIVE GPA, THEY NEED TO SAY:

NYEMA

WE'LL SEE YOU NEXT SEMESTER!

JAMILA

WILL THEY LIKE ME?
AND BRING ME INTO THEIR EXCLUSIVE CIRCLE
OF FRIENDS?
IS IT LIKELY

JAMILA (CONT)
THEY WILL SEE ME AND DECIDE THAT THEY
MUST LET ME IN?

MAKE ME BEAUTIFUL.
MAKE ME IN-DEMAND.
MAKE ME STEP INTO THAT ROOM IN FULL
COMMAND.

MAKE THEM SEE MY WORTH.
MAKE THEM SAY I'M IT.
MAKE THEM OFFER A SCHOLARSHIP.

MAKE ME UNDENIABLE, UNDENIABLE.
UNDENIABLE. THE MOST DESIRABLE.
UNDENIABLE, UNDENIABLE.
UNDENIABLE, UNDENIABLE.

NYEMA
I got it. We doin' braids: simple, clean, but powerful. When
I'm finished, you're gonna get into North Tech,
Princeton...you'll even score a date with that boy you've had
your eyes on.

JAMILA
Who, Marcus?

NYEMA
Don't you "Who, Marcus" me. I seen't you stalking him on
IG try'na slide in them DM's. You ain't slick. Just let me
know if he has a cute older brother.

JAMILA
Too bad he won't stop talking about Harper Tisdale.

NYEMA

Girl please, one look at you and Marcus will be saying
"Harper Tisdale who?"

> *(NYEMA sits JAMILA in her chair. JAMILA*
> *holds a jar of hair gel as NYEMA starts braiding*
> *the back of her hair..)*

NYEMA

WATCH ME WORK MY MAGIC ON THIS HEAD OF
YOURS,
I ALREADY CAN TELL
THE MICRO BRAIDS WILL SO DISPLAY
YOUR EYES AND FACIAL FEATURES WELL.

JAMILA

JUST KEEP MY EDGES LOOSE 'CAUSE
MY HEAD CAN'T TAKE ABUSE.

NYEMA

ARE YOU SURE?
THAT COULD GIVE YOU PROBLEMS.

JAMILA

JUST MAKE SURE THEY'RE NOT TOO TIGHT.

NYEMA

I'LL GET YOU RIGHT.
TRUST ME, YOU'LL LOOK AWESOME.

JAMILA
WILL THEY NOTICE
ALL OF THE EFFORT I PUT IN MY HAIR TO
ENHANCE?
DO THEY KNOW THIS?
ALL OF THE WORK KNOWING I'M ONLY GIVEN
ONE CHANCE!

MAKE ME BEAUTIFUL.
MAKE ME IN-DEMAND.
MAKE ME STEP INTO THAT ROOM IN FULL
COMMAND.

MAKE THEM SEE MY WORTH.
MAKE THEM SAY I'M IT.
MAKE THEM OFFER A SCHOLARSHIP.

NYEMA
I'LL MAKE YOU...

NYEMA/JAMILA
UNDENIABLE, UNDENIABLE, UNDENIABLE.

JAMILA
THE MOST DESIRABLE.

NYEMA/JAMILA
UNDENIABLE, UNDENIABLE, UNDENIABLE.

NYEMA
I'LL MAKE YOU UNDENIABLE.

(Scene transitions to JAMILA'S fantasy world at school. FULL COMPANY enters.)

6

JAMILA
ALL OF MY LIFE I DONE BEEN
SEARCHING A MOMENT TO WIN.
'CAUSE OF MY DARK SKIN,
I HAD IT HARD AND
DIDN'T HAVE A LOT OF FRIENDS.
CALLED EVERY NAME IN THE BOOK:
"DARK AND UGLY", FELT LIKE A TARGET.
KIDS PETTING MY HAIR LIKE AN ANIMAL
SAYING "IT FEELS LIKE CARPET."
SO I READ BOOKS, MADE STRAIGHT A'S,
AND STAYED AWAY FROM THE DRAMA.
ALL I HAD WAS ME AND MY HAIR,
AND MICHELLE OBAMA.
ANOINTED WITH HER ENERGY INTO ME,
SPIRITUALLY, I AM IN TACT.
I AM NOT BROKEN, NOT OUT OF WHACK,
I WILL NOT CRACK LIKE SKIN THAT IS BLACK.
I SEE MY FUTURE IN FRONT OF ME
AS I WONDER WHAT WILL BECOME OF ME.
WITH MICHELLE AS MY ONLY COMPANY.

(Holding her Michelle Obama book tightly.)

JAMILA
COLLEGE IS THE ONLY PLACE I WANT TO BE.

*(The FULL COMPANY circles JAMILA as
NYEMA puts the finishing touches on her hair.)*

JAMILA	**FULL COMPANY**
BEAUTIFUL HAIR: IT	AHHHH.
STARTS WITH	AHHHH.
BEAUTIFUL HAIR.	AHHHH.
IT STARTS WITH	AHHHH.
BEAUTIFUL HAIR.	
IT STARTS WITH	
BEAUTIFUL,	
BEAUTIFUL, BEAUTIFUL	
HAIR.	

FULL COMPANY
BEAUTIFUL, BEAUTIFUL, BEAUTIFUL HAIR.
BEAUTIFUL, BEAUTIFUL, BEAUTIFUL HAIR.

(The FULL COMPANY opens up and JAMILA'S finished braids are revealed. The STUDENTS also show off their vast array of black hairstyles on girls and boys alike: cornrows, defined curls, high buns, ponytails, deadlocks, afro-puffs, short knots, twists, caesars, 360 waves, mohawks, high top fades, etc.)

JAMILA
I AM...

JAMILA/FULL COMPANY
BEAUTIFUL!

JAMILA
I AM...

JAMILA/FULL COMPANY
IN-DEMAND!

JAMILA

I WILL...

JAMILA/FULL COMPANY
STEP INTO THAT ROOM IN FULL COMMAND!

JAMILA

THEY WILL...

JAMILA/FULL COMPANY
SEE MY WORTH! THEY WILL...

JAMILA/FULL COMPANY
SAY I'M IT!

JAMILA

THEY WILL...

JAMILA/FULL COMPANY
OFFER A SCHOLARSHIP!

JAMILA/FULL COMPANY
I AM UNDENIABLE, UNDENIABLE.
UNDENIABLE. THE MOST DESIRABLE.
UNDENIABLE, UNDENIABLE.
UNDENIABLE. UNDENIABLE.

JAMILA	FULL COMPANY
UNDENIABLE.	LOOK AT HER, LOOK AT
UNDENIABLE.	HER BEAUTIFUL HAIR
UNDENIABLE.	HER BEAUTIFUL HAIR
	EVERYBODY LOOK AT
	HER BEAUTIFUL HAIR!
	LOOK AT HER, LOOK AT
	HER BEAUTIFUL HAIR
	HER BEAUTIFUL HAIR
	EVERYBODY LOOK AT
	HER BEAUTIFUL HAIR!
	LOOK AT HER, LOOK AT
	HER BEAUTIFUL HAIR
	HER BEAUTIFUL HAIR
	EVERYBODY LOOK AT
	HER BEAUTIFUL HAIR!

FULL COMPANY
LOOK AT HER, LOOK AT HER BEAUTIFUL HAIR
HER BEAUTIFUL HAIR
EVERYBODY LOOK AT HER BEAUTIFUL HAIR!

JAMILA
UNDENIABLE!

END SONG.

(JAMILA is no longer in her fantasy world. The scene has fully transitioned into SCHOOL. The bell rings and STUDENTS disperse. She looks around to find no one paying attention to her. MARCUS enters.)

SCENE 2: SCHOOL - HALLWAY, THE NEXT DAY

MARCUS
Yo J! Come through with the fresh braids!

JAMILA
Thanks Marcus. Just trying to look cute for my North Tech interview today. It's really going to be practice for Princeton.

MARCUS
Nice! You definitely got the cute part down.

JAMILA
You sure know how to make a girl feel good about herself.

MARCUS
Of course. That's what friends are for.

JAMILA
Right...friends...of course. About that: I was actually wondering if...

(HARPER enters.)

HARPER
(Interrupting, ignoring JAMILA.)
Hey Marcus!

MARCUS
Harper! What up Beautiful!

HARPER
Did you notice anything different about me today?

MARCUS
(Earnestly.)

Nope.

HARPER

I have a pink accent nail. Cute, right?

JAMILA
(Under her breath.)

Basic.

MARCUS

Yea. And it's on the wedding ring finger. Sweet.

> *(As HARPER and MARCUS talk, Jamila grows increasingly annoyed.)*

HARPER

Oh, you noticed!

MARCUS

Of course I did!

HARPER

Everybody's doing it. It gives that ring finger just a little more pop.

MARCUS

I love a pop. No cap: your fashion game has always been A-1.

HARPER

I know, right? So, I was thinking maybe you and I get together later this afternoon? After my interview for North Tech?

MARCUS

It's a date. See you then Gorgeous. *(Begins to leave)* Later J. *(Stops.)* Wait...you were about to tell me something...?

JAMILA

Oh...I was wondering...*(a beat)*...how I got such a great friend in you!

MARCUS

I know, right? I'm pretty amazing. Not to toot my own horn but...

MARCUS/JAMILA

"Toot toot"!

> *(MARCUS and JAMILA laugh at their obvious inside joke. Now Harper is annoyed.)*

MARCUS

You may wanna let some of this Marcus-swag rub off on ya - may help you with getting into Princeton!

> *(JAMILA laughs.)*

JAMILA

Listen, I'll take what I can get!

MARCUS

Peace ya'll!

JAMILA/HARPER

Bye Marcus.

> *(He exits. HARPER'S friends join in on the conversation.)*

HARPER

Princeton, huh? Interesting.

JAMILA

Yep. Also interviewing for North Tech. Just want to have options, you know?

HARPER

My Mom graduated with the Head of Admissions, so I'm practically a shoo-in. I don't need options.

JAMILA

Must be nice.

HARPER

It is, actually. *(A beat.)* Allow me to share some wisdom from an insider's perspective.

JAMILA

That's so thoughtful of you Harper but I really didn't ask...

HARPER

Braids are a little inappropriate for this.

HARPER FRIEND 1

I'd go with a more professional style.

HARPER FRIEND 2

You wanna look more put together.

HARPER FRIEND 3

More presentable.

HARPER

Exactly. But it's your life. Do as you please.

JAMILA

Yeah, there is something I wanna do, but that may ruin my chances in admissions even more.

HARPER

Someone's a little spicy this morning. Didn't mean to offend. It's just my sworn duty as the most popular girl in school to lead our student body with grace. You're welcome.

JAMILA

We all have room to grow.

HARPER

Speak for yourself.

SONG: "CLASS IN SESSION"

HARPER
I'M BAD AND BEAUTIFUL TO MY CUTICLES.
BOYS TRY'NA HOLLA AT ME IS USUAL.
I'M THE PROTAGONIST IN THIS MUSICAL.
MOST POPULAR, THAT'S INDISPUTABLE.
I AM A DIVA WHO GETS WHAT SHE WANTS.

STUDENTS

WHAT!

HARPER
NO WAITING IN LINE, I JUST SKIP TO THE FRONT.

STUDENTS

WHAT!

HARPER
QUEEN OF THE COOL-TABLE, WATCH HOW I STUNT:

STUDENTS
WHAT!

HARPER
THE HAIR, THE SHOES, THE NAILS, THE STRUT.

STUDENTS
WHAT!

HARPER
THROUGHOUT THE YEARS I HAVE NOTICED A TREND...

STUDENTS
WHOA!

HARPER
SOME LACK THE SWAGGER AND SO THEY PRETEND.

STUDENTS
WHOA!

HARPER
I KNOW THAT IT'S TOUGH, BUT I MAKE IT LOOK SIMPLE.

STUDENTS
WHOA!

HARPER
IT'S ONLY RIGHT I HELP YOU REACH YOUR
POTENTIAL.

STUDENTS
WHOA!

HARPER
THIS IS MY QUEENDOM AND I RUN THE
SCHOOL.
THE WEBSTER'S DEFINITION OF WHAT'S COOL.

STUDENTS
WHOA!

HARPER
CAUTIOUS OF WHO I INVITE.
SO MANY HATERS, I MUST BE DOING
SOMETHING RIGHT!

STUDENTS
A'IGHT!

HARPER
STEP BACK AND DON'T GET TOO...

HARPER/STUDENTS
CLOSE.

HARPER
BETTER BOW DOWN WHEN YOU...

HARPER/STUDENTS
APPROACH.

HARPER
GET CHA PEN AND PAPER AND TAKE...

HARPER/STUDENTS
NOTES:
CLASS IS IN SESSION!

HARPER
I DON'T MEAN TO BRAG OR...

HARPER/STUDENTS
BOAST.

HARPER
I'M LYIN' I'M THE QUEEN WITH THE...

HARPER/STUDENTS
MOST.

HARPER
I DO IT BIG EVERY TIK TOK...

HARPER/STUDENTS
POST.
CLASS IS IN SESSION.
CLASS IS IN SESSION.
CLASS IS IN SESSION.
CLASS IS IN SESSION.
CLASS IS IN SESSION.

*(Dance break. JAMILA watches HARPER glide
through the hallway in awe.)*

JAMILA

WHAT IS IT LIKE TO GLIDE THROUGH THE
HALLWAYS
KNOWING YOU ARE MISS POPULAR?
I WANT TO GLIDE THROUGH LIFE LIKE HARPER
BECAUSE EVERYONE FLOCKS TO HER.

(MARCUS enters and dances with HARPER. As
this happens, JAMILA stands to side and
observes.)

JAMILA

MAKE HIM NOTICE ME.
MAKE HIM FALL IN LOVE.
MAKE ME BE THE ONLY GIRL HE'S THINKING
OF.

MAKE HIM LOOK AT ME
THE WAY HE LOOKS AT HER
MAKE ME BE THE ONE HE'D PREFER.

JAMILA

MAKE ME...

JAMILA/STUDENTS

UNDENIABLE. UNDENIABLE.
UNDENIABLE.

JAMILA

UNDENIABLE.

STUDENTS
(Dancing with HARPER.)
SHE'S UNDENIABLE. UNDENIABLE.
SHE'S UNDENIABLE. UNDENIABLE.

(MARCUS exits.)

HARPER
SO JAMILA - HERE'S WHAT I'LL GIVE YA:
COUPLE OF TIPS YOU SHOULD CONSIDER.
A GIRL LIKE ME - ALWAYS A WINNER.
MOVE LIKE A PRO, NEVER BEGINNER.

HARPER/STUDENTS
STEP BACK AND DON'T GET TOO CLOSE.
BETTER BOW DOWN WHEN YOU APPROACH.
GET CHA PEN AND PAPER AND TAKE NOTES:
CLASS IS IN SESSION!

I DON'T MEAN TO BRAG OR BOAST.
NAH, I'M LYIN' I'M THE QUEEN WITH THE MOST.
I DO IT BIG EVERY TIK TOK POST.
CLASS IS IN SESSION.
CLASS IS IN SESSION.
CLASS IS IN SESSION.
CLASS IS IN SESSION.
CLASS IS IN SESSION!

END SONG.

<u>SCENE 3 - HALLWAY, AFTER SCHOOL, LATE</u>
<u>AFTERNOON</u>

> *(JAMILA waits outside of the conference room,*
> *pacing nervously back and forth holding her*
> *Michelle Obama book. MARCUS enters.)*

MARCUS

Yo J - you good?

JAMILA

I'm freaking out. I thought I'd be cool and relaxed with this
interview. I mean, it's just North Tech, right? How tough can
it be? But I'm like...shook!

MARCUS

Sometimes it's good to have a little nervous energy. Means
you're alive! *(Noticing her book.)* I'm sure Michelle would
tell you to think of who you're *Becoming*...!

JAMILA

I see what you did there.

MARCUS

Am I lying?

JAMILA

No, you're right. She's great for situations like this.

MARCUS

And as Barack would say: *(ala Barack Obama)* "Jamila..we
did not come to fear the future. We came here to shape it."

> *(JAMILA laughs.)*

MARCUS

She laughs! *(Announces to the room.)* I got Jamila to laugh ya'll! She's laughing!

JAMILA

Thanks. North Tech is supposed to be the exhibition before the big game: Princeton.

MARCUS

Hey, North Tech is also a pretty tough school to get into.

JAMILA

I think I'm nervous my GPA won't be enough for them.

MARCUS

Well that's your first problem.

JAMILA

What?

SONG: "LIKE A SISTER"

MARCUS
YOU WORRY ABOUT THINGS
BEYOND YOUR CONTROL.
'THOUGH I UNDERSTAND THE URGE,
YOU GOTTA LET IT GO.
YOU'LL DRIVE YOURSELF CRAZY GOING BACK
AND FORTH
WITH HYPOTHETICAL SITUATIONS.
IT'S A MUST YOU STAY PATIENT.
JAMILA, YOU'RE THE MOST KIND,
YOU'RE THE MOST DRIVEN PERSON I KNOW.
I NEVER WORRY ABOUT YOU.
YOU WILL BE FINE WHERE EVER YOU CHOOSE
TO GO.

JAMILA

Thanks Marcus. You're always there when I need you.

MARCUS

Of course I am.

> *(The more MARCUS sings, the more smitten
> JAMILA becomes. They slowly move closer
> towards one another.)*

MARCUS

YOU MEAN THE WORLD TO ME.
SINCE ELEMENTARY I COULDN'T RESIST YA.
I WANT THE WORLD TO SEE
EVERYTHING I SEE. J, YOU'RE...LIKE...

> *(They stand face to face, close enough to kiss.)*

JAMILA

Yeah...?

MARCUS

...A...SISTER!

JAMILA

Excuse me?

MARCUS

A sister!

JAMILA

Your sister? Like...your...

MARCUS

Yeah! You know, like the homie. My bestie.

JAMILA

Of course I am.

MARCUS

YOU'RE LIKE ONE OF THE HOMIES I CAN
ALWAYS KICK IT WITH.
YOU'RE LIKE MY FAMILY, SO SWEET AND
INNOCENT.
YOU'RE LIKE THAT ONE FRIEND THAT I'VE
KNOWN SO LONG
IF WE EVER THOUGHT ABOUT DATING WE'D
KNOW IT'D BE WRONG.
YOU CAN'T NAME A BETTER DUO.
ANYBODY YOU KNOW:
CARLTON AND WILL. MICKEY, PLUTO.
SCULLY AND MULDER, JACK AND LIZ LEMON.
WOODY AND BUZZ LIGHTYEAR!

JAMILA

YUP, I GET IT!

MARCUS

YOU'RE LIKE MY LIL' COUSIN, BUT CLOSER.
I'M YOUR BIG BRO LOOKIN' OVER YOUR
SHOULDER

JAMILA

I'M DEFINITELY OLDER.

MARCUS

YOU'RE LIKE MY BUDDY, MY ACE WHO CAN'T
BE REPLACED.
GIRLS WOULD NEED YOUR APPROVAL IF THEY
EVER WANNA DATE.

JAMILA

GREAT.

MARCUS

YOU'RE MY BEST FRIEND.
NOTHING LESS THAN.
AND IF I GOT MARRIED YOU WOULD BE MY
BEST MAN.
ANYTIME WE'RE APART - I MISS YA.
YEAH, I GOT THREE BROTHERS AT HOME BUT
JAMILA...

MARCUS

YOU'RE LIKE A SISTER:
THE ONE I GOTTA LOOK OUT FOR.
I WILL PROTECT YOU FOR SURE.
YOU'RE LIKE A SISTER:
I GOT YA BACK, BELIEVE THAT.
YOU KNOW I STAY DOWN LIKE FOUR FLATS!
YOU ARE MY HOMIE, MY BUDDY, MY BFF,
MY COMPADRE FOR LIFE
NOTHING MORE, NOTHING LESS.
LAST THING I EVER WANNA SEE IS YOU
STRESSED,
SO I'MA FIGHT TIL THERE'S NOTHING LEFT.
YOU'RE LIKE A SISTER!

*(MARCUS gives JAMILA a big hug and pats her
on the back. JAMILA reluctantly hugs him back.
A STUDENT enters and notices them.)*

STUDENT

Aw, you guys look so cute together. You make a great
couple!

MARCUS
(Laughing.)
Ew! No way! We're practically related!

STUDENT
Oh, sorry.

(STUDENT exits.)

MARCUS
That's so funny, right? Can you imagine? You and I: boyfriend and girlfriend? That's comedy!

JAMILA
Yeah...comedy...

IMAGINE YOU AND I GOING STEADY
TOGETHER LIKE ROMEO AND JULIET...

MARCUS
I'M GAGGING ALREADY!

JAMILA
RIGHT. IMAGINE US WRITING POEMS LIKE
LOVE BIRDS.

MARCUS
THAT'S THE CRAZIEST THING I EVER HEARD!

JAMILA
IMAGINE US: HIT BY CUPID'S ARROW.
I'M QUEEN OF EGYPT, YOU ARE MY...

MARCUS
PHARAOH.

JAMILA/MARCUS

HOLDING HANDS...

JAMILA

AND NEVER LOOKING AWAY.
IMAGINE ACTUALLY LOOKING FORWARD TO
VALENTINE'S DAY.

> *(JAMILA and MARCUS hold hands, but realize
> they are too close and let go immediately.)*

JAMILA

Well thanks for the support. I should get ready for my
interview.

MARCUS

Not with that attitude.

JAMILA

What do you mean?

MARCUS

We gotta loosen you up and get you right! Follow me.

> *(MARCUS does a couple of dance steps to get
> JAMILA to calm her nerves. At first she is
> apprehensive, then she finally can't resist and
> joins in. They dance.)*

MARCUS

LOOSEN IT UP A LITTLE BIT.

JAMILA

I don't think so.

MARCUS
LOOSEN IT UP A LITTLE BIT, A LITTLE BIT.

JAMILA
I look ridiculous!

MARCUS
LOOSEN IT UP A LITTLE BIT. A LITTLE BIT.
LOOSEN IT UP A LITTLE BIT, A LITTLE BIT.

JAMILA
Fine.

MARCUS
LOOSEN IT UP!

(HARPER enters, but MARCUS and JAMILA can't see her. HARPER spies on them.)

MARCUS/JAMILA
LOOSEN IT UP A LITTLE BIT.
LOOSEN IT UP A LITTLE BIT, A LITTLE BIT.
LOOSEN IT UP A LITTLE BIT. A LITTLE BIT.
LOOSEN IT UP A LITTLE BIT, A LITTLE BIT.
LOOSEN IT UP!

JAMILA
EVEN WHEN I GET OVERLY NERVOUS
YOU STILL MAKE ME LAUGH AND REMIND ME
OF MY PURPOSE
YOU'RE SO EARNEST. REALLY, I DON'T
DESERVE THIS.

MARCUS

YOU WALK INTO THAT ROOM AND ACT LIKE YOU
EARNED THIS.
I'VE KNOWN YOU LONGER THAN ANYONE.
IF THERE'S ANYTHING I KNOW ABOUT YOU IS
AT ANYTIME YOU'LL GET IT DONE!
CUT FROM THE SAME CLOTH, GO FIGURE.
I'M IN YOUR CORNER ROOTING FOR YA -
'CAUSE...

YOU'RE LIKE A SISTER:
THE ONE I GOTTA LOOK OUT FOR.
I WILL PROTECT YOU FOR SURE.
YOU'RE LIKE A SISTER:
I GOT YA BACK, BELIEVE THAT
YOU KNOW I STAY DOWN LIKE FOUR FLATS!
YOU ARE MY HOMIE, MY BUDDY, MY BFF,
MY COMPADRE FOR LIFE
NOTHING MORE, NOTHING LESS.
LAST THING I EVER WANNA SEE IS YOU
STRESSED
SO I'MA FIGHT TIL THERE'S NOTHING LEFT.
MY SISTER!

YOU GOT THIS SIS - I BELIEVE IN YOU.
COBB TECH WILL SEE EVERYTHING I SEE IN YOU.
BE YOURSELF AND GREATNESS WILL BE
DISCOVERED.
AND WHEN YOU GET NERVOUS, REMEMBER
YOUR BIG BROTHER.

LOOSEN IT UP A LITTLE BIT.
LOOSEN IT UP A LITTLE BIT, A LITTLE BIT.
LOOSEN IT UP A LITTLE BIT. A LITTLE BIT.
LOOSEN IT UP A LITTLE BIT, A LITTLE BIT.
LOOSEN IT UP!

JAMILA

LOOSEN IT UP A LITTLE BIT.
LOOSEN IT UP A LITTLE BIT, A LITTLE BIT.

> *(MARCUS exits. JAMILA continues to dance on
> her own. HARPER laughs to herself, pulls out
> her phone and records her while she dances.)*

JAMILA

LOOSEN IT UP A LITTLE BIT. A LITTLE BIT.
LOOSEN IT UP A LITTLE BIT, A LITTLE BIT.
LOOSEN IT UP!

END SONG.

> *(JAMILA sings and dances to herself, snapping
> her fingers on the 1 and the 3. From a distance
> her dance could be read as suggestive. HARPER
> enters with her cell phone and films her.
> JAMILA stops.)*

HARPER

Little rhythmic advice: try snapping on the two and four.
Makes it less awkward looking.

JAMILA

What are you going to do with that video?

HARPER

Send it to North Tech and let them judge you.

> *(JAMILA is quiet.)*

30

HARPER

Relax, it was just a joke. Besides, you have bigger worries.
Those braids ain't cuttin' it.

(INTERVIEWER 1 enters with a clipboard.)

INTERVIEWER 1

Harper Tisdale? You're up.

(HARPER follows the INTERVIEWER.)

HARPER

Watch how it's done.

*(HARPER walks in the room with the
INTERVIEWER. They shut the door and
embrace.)*

HARPER

SONG: "THE INTERVIEW "

INTERVIEWER 1

WELL, HI HARPER!

HARPER

HI!

INTERVIEWER 1

HOW'S YOUR FAMILY DOING?

HARPER

WELL, MOM AND DAD SEND THEIR REGARDS,
HAPPY THAT I'M INTERVIEWING.

INTERVIEWER 1
GOOD! THIS INTERVIEW'S A FORMALITY
THOUGH, WE KNOW YOU'RE ACCEPTED,
NATURALLY.

HARPER
NATURALLY, AND I ACCEPT HAPPILY.
BUT RIGHT, THERE'S QUESTIONS YOU MUST
ASK OF ME.

INTERVIEWER 1
RIGHT. WHY ARE YOU INTERESTED IN NORTH
TECH?

HARPER
WELL MOM AND DAD WENT, PLUS YOU'RE
CUTTING THE CHECK.

INTERVIEWER 1
AH YES, GOTTA LOVE A FULL SCHOLARSHIP.
WHO NEEDS TO LOOK AT OTHER COLLEGES?
AND WHAT IS YOUR GPA?

HARPER
I WOULD SAY A PRETTY SOLID TWO POINT
EIGHT.

INTERVIEWER 1
GREAT! AND TELL ME YOUR STRENGTHS.

HARPER
I'M BAD AND BEAUTIFUL
TO MY CUTICLES
IS THAT SUITABLE?

INTERVIEWER 1

I DON'T NEED TO HEAR ANYMORE!
I DON'T NEED TO HEAR ANYMORE!
YOU ARE A GEM!
YOU ARE THE STUDENT WE'VE BEEN LOOKING
FOR,
SO TELL YOUR MOM AND DAD YOU ARE IN!

HARPER

YES!

INTERVIEWER 1

I DON'T NEED TO HEAR ANYMORE!
I DON'T NEED TO HEAR ANYMORE!
NOTHING AT ALL!
BESIDES MOM AND DAD - KEEP THIS TO
YOURSELF.
HARPER: I'LL SEE YOU NEXT FALL!

*(Lights down on INTERVIEWER 1. The Scene
transitions back outside the room.)*

HARPER

YA'LL!
I made it! North Tech, here I come! Thank you!

(FRIENDS applaud and congratulate her.)

HARPER
(To JAMILA.)
Good luck Jamila, you'll certainly need it.

(INTERVIEWER 1 re-enters.)

INTERVIEWER 1

Ja...uh...Ja-'mile-ah? Watkins?

JAMILA
Jamila Watkins.

INTERVIEWER 1
Right. This way.

JAMILA - IS THAT NAME ON YOUR BIRTH
CERTIFICATE?

JAMILA
UHH...YEAH, IT'S PRETTY LEGITIMATE.

INTERVIEWER 1
WELL THAT'S QUITE A UNIQUE NAME, ISN'T IT?
DO YOU GO BY A NICKNAME?

JAMILA
THAT'S INSIGNIFICANT. MY GPA...

INTERVIEWER 1
(Interrupting.)
IS THAT HOW YOU NORMALLY WEAR YOUR
HAIR?
SEEMS INAPPROPRIATE FOR HERE.
YOU WEARING EXTENSIONS OR IS THAT REAL?

JAMILA
DOES IT MAKE A DIFFERENCE?

INTERVIEWER 1
ONE'S NOT IDEAL.

JAMILA
WELL IF YOU CHECK OUT MY TRANSCRIPT
YOU WILL READ THAT
I MADE STRAIGHT A'S SINCE NINTH GRADE...

INTERVIEWER 1

I SEE THAT.
BUT CAN I OFFER FEEDBACK?

JAMILA

SURE.

INTERVIEWER 1

YOU LACK EXTRACURRICULAR ACTIVITIES
AND YOU NEED THAT.
I SEE YOUR GRADES ALL IN YOUR FILE.
BUT HOW DO I KNOW YOU'D GO THE EXTRA
MILE?
PERHAPS IF YOU PUSHED YOURSELF A BIT
MORE -
THAT WOULD GET YOU IN THE DOOR.

JAMILA

WOW.

INTERVIEWER 1

I DON'T NEED TO HEAR ANYMORE!
I DON'T NEED TO HEAR ANYMORE!
I HAVE WHAT I NEED.
YOU ARE A STUDENT WHO HAS SOME
POTENTIAL
THOUGH I'M NOT SURE HOW WE'LL PROCEED.

JAMILA

SURE.

INTERVIEWER 1

I DON'T NEED TO HEAR ANYMORE!

JAMILA

ANYTHING ELSE TO EXPLORE?

INTERVIEWER 1

THAT IS OKAY.
WE WILL BE IN TOUCH IN A FEW WEEKS.
FOR NOW, HAVE A NICE DAY.

JAMILA

OKAY.

(Lights down on the INTERVIEWER. The Scene transitions back outside the room. HARPER approaches JAMILA.)

HARPER

GOSH, I HATE ALWAYS BEING RIGHT.
MAYBE YOU SHOULD'VE LISTENED.
MAYBE YOU SHOULDN'T HAVE WORN THE
BRAIDS LIKE I SAID.
I HATE TO POUR MORE SALT IN THE WOUND:
THERE'S ALWAYS COMMUNITY COLLEGE!
SORRY, TOO SOON?

END SONG.

<u>SCENE 4: SCHOOL, FOLLOWING WEEK</u>

> *(JAMILA and MARCUS sit in the living room while NYEMA gathers her belongings.)*

NYEMA

Sorry about the interviews, sis.

JAMILA

I can't even get into North Tech. What business do I have interviewing for Princeton?

NYEMA

How do you know if they rejected you if they haven't sent a letter yet?

JAMILA

They told Harper on the spot, didn't they?

MARCUS

They did but...

JAMILA

See. Exactly.

NYEMA

You can't compare yourself to her.

MARCUS

She's right.

NYEMA

(To MARCUS.) Thank you. Sidebar: Jamila tells me you have three brothers?

MARCUS

Yeah!

JAMILA

Okay, time for you to go Nyema.

NYEMA

And are they older?

MARCUS

Yeah!

JAMILA

Bye Nyema!

> *(As NYEMA walks out the front door, she mouths
> and gestures JAMILA to "go for it" with
> MARCUS. JAMILA shuts the door.)*

MARCUS

Your sister's right, you know. You can't compare yourself to
Harper. You gotta run your own race.

> *(A beat.)*

JAMILA

Do you really like her? Like...*like her*, like her?

MARCUS

I dunno. She *is* pretty hot!

JAMILA

Right.

> *(MARCUS notices JAMILA isn't amused by his
> joke.)*

MARCUS

No seriously, jokes aside. I like her confidence. It's attractive.

JAMILA

I can see that.

MARCUS

Speaking of confidence - I have an idea for you.

JAMILA

For me?

MARCUS

That's right. You're going to run for Student Body President.

JAMILA

Says who?

MARCUS

Says your resume!

JAMILA

Listen, I'm usually down for your wacky ideas but that ain't happening.

MARCUS

North Tech said you lack extracurricular activities. What's a better look than Student Body President?

JAMILA

It's just a popularity contest.

MARCUS

A popularity contest you're gonna win, with my assistance. It'll be just in time for Princeton.

JAMILA

Sorry Marcus, not this time.

MARCUS

Hey! W-W-M-D!

JAMILA

What?

MARCUS

W-W-M-D: What would Michelle do?!

JAMILA

I don't know, probably hit the gym!

MARCUS

J, all you do is talk about how strong Michelle Obama is. Do you think Michelle would sit here feeling sorry for herself?

JAMILA

Who knows!

SONG: "WHAT WOULD MICHELLE DO?"

MARCUS

We know good and well Michelle would walk out there in full black girl magic with a dope fit, hair laid, and them arms and she would turn this whole situation around quicker than you can say Obama!

C-C-C-COME ON, COME ON IT'S TIME TO TAKE A SHOT.
IT'S TIME TO HIT COLLEGE WITH EVERYTHING WE GOT.
IF YOU WANNA SUCCEED AND MAKE THE DREAM COME TRUE.

MARCUS (CONT)
I GOTTA ASK YOU: WHAT WOULD MICHELLE
DO?

L-L-L-LEGGO, LEGGO, WE'RE REVING UP TO
RUN
FOR STUDENT BODY PRESIDENT, SO MUCH
WORK TO BE DONE.
AND IF PRINCETON'S THE SCHOOL YOU WANNA
GET INTO
YOU GOTTA THINK BOO: WHAT WOULD
MICHELLE DO?

MICHELLE WOULDN'T SULK OR SAY "OH WOE
IS ME"
MICHELLE WOULD BE FLAWLESS AS FLAWLESS
CAN BE.
MICHELLE WOULDN'T MOPE, OH NO SHE
WOULDN'T POUT.
MICHELLE WOULD STAND TALL AND REMOVE
ANY DOUBT.

G-G-G-GET UP, GET OUT GET DOWN AND TAKE A
CHANCE
I GUARANTEE ADMISSION WHEN THEY TAKE A
GLANCE.
HOW ELSE YOU GONNA WOW 'EM IN THAT
INTERVIEW?
I'LL GIVE YOU ONE CLUE: WHAT WOULD
MICHELLE DO?

JAMILA
But I don't know the first thing about being a President.

MARCUS

Sure you do! You just gotta talk to the people and say something presidential!

JAMILA

You mean something like: *(Doing her best presidential voice.)* "For me this issue is personal."

MARCUS

Exactly! And you don't even have to mean what you say, you just have to sound like you mean it.

JAMILA

Oh, well that's easy! You mean like, "I'm worried about Main Street, not Wall Street!"

MARCUS

You're a natural! But you gotta channel Michelle. Conjure up the spirit of Michelle. The voice, the charisma, the vibe. If it were Michelle giving a speech, how would she do it?

JAMILA

WE'LL TAKE IT HIGH WHEN THEY GO LOW.

MARCUS

Yeah! That's how you do it!

JAMILA

WE'LL TAKE IT HIGH WHEN THEY GO LOW.

(STUDENTS gather around JAMILA.)

JAMILA/STUDENTS

WE'LL GO HIGH WHEN THEY GO LOW!
WE'LL GO HIGH WHEN THEY GO LOW!

JAMILA

LET ME BE CLEAR: WE NEED STRONGER
LEADERSHIP.
WE NEED A NEW PLAN IN ACTION AND WE
NEED IT QUICK!
I BELIEVE THIS TRUTH IS SELF-EVIDENT.
SO VOTE JAMILA FOR STUDENT BODY
PRESIDENT!

JAMILA	**STUDENTS**
WE'LL TAKE IT HIGH	LET US BE CLEAR: WE
WHEN THEY GO LOW.	NEED STRONGER
WE'LL TAKE IT HIGH	LEADERSHIP.
WHEN THEY GO LOW.	WE NEED A NEW PLAN
	IN ACTION AND WE
	NEED IT QUICK.
	WE BELIEVE THIS
	TRUTH IS SELF-
	EVIDENT.
	SO VOTE JAMILA FOR
	STUDENT BODY
	PRESIDENT.

*(Scene transitions to JAMILA and MARCUS
handing out flyers to the STUDENTS, who are
impressed About a month has passed in time.)*

MARCUS

And just like that - you're the front runner to win!

JAMILA

Ha! Just like that.

MARCUS

And to think: about a month ago you were telling me "it's just a popularity contest!" And here we are. Hate to say I told you so.

JAMILA

I know, I know. Thank you.

MARCUS

Don't thank me. Thank Michelle. All it takes is a little confidence.

JAMILA

Well, while I'm channeling Michelle, I think it's only right I acknowledge my Barack. Thank you!

> *(JAMILA gives MARCUS a hug, then realizes they're sharing an intimate moment. HARPER enters, but MARCUS and JAMILA cannot see her. HARPER spies on them.)*

MARCUS

Oooohhh bama...

> *(A beat. They lean in towards each other to kiss, but MARCUS pulls away. He kneels down and picks up a piece of JAMILA'S braided hair.)*

MARCUS

Hey, I think this fell out...

> *(Hands her the braid.)*

JAMILA

Oh my God.

(HARPER enters with her FRIENDS holding another one of JAMILA'S braids.)

HARPER

Ew Jamila, there's little pieces of you all over school!

HARPER FRIEND 1

So gross!

HARPER FRIEND 2

I guess her Mom can't afford to buy her good hair!

(They laugh. JAMILA runs out.)

MARCUS

Would you stop it already?

HARPER

Lighten up Marcus, we're just having fun.

MARCUS

Whatever. Jamila!

(MARCUS exits after JAMILA.)

HARPER FRIEND 3

Bad weave ain't a good look if you're running for Student Body President.

HARPER FRIEND 2

I would so quit if I were her!

HARPER

I think now's a good time to kick things up a notch and put my name in the hat!

(HARPER pulls out her phone and records herself. STUDENTS enter, staring at their phones, watching a HARPER'S social media post.)

HARPER
(Via social media post.)
My fellow classmates, it is with great pleasure I've decided to run for Student Body President. I believe we need a more appropriate candidate in every aspect. Jamila Watkins? Seriously, we can do better. She can't even keep hair on her own body, imagine her trying to run the student body!

HARPER
Jamila says she has big dreams of one day making it into Princeton. Ha! Can you imagine? I don't claim to be an expert but I do know that Ivy League schools tend to frown on inappropriate behavior like this...

(HARPER'S video of JAMILA suggestively dancing flashes across the screen. The ENSEMBLE react, giggle, type comments on their phones, etc.)

HARPER
How embarrassing!

(The STUDENTS react, laughing, typing comments in their phones. The video gains thousands of views.)

STUDENTS
LET US BE CLEAR: WE NEED STRONGER LEADERSHIP
WE NEED A NEW PLAN IN ACTION AND WE NEED IT QUICK

STUDENTS (CONT)
WE BELIEVE THIS TRUTH IS SELF-EVIDENT.
SO VOTE HARPER FOR STUDENT BODY
PRESIDENT
VOTE HARPER FOR STUDENT BODY PRESIDENT.
VOTE HARPER FOR STUDENT BODY PRESIDENT!

(MARCUS enters.)

MARCUS
YOU GO HIGH WHEN THEY GO LOW.

END SONG.

*(JAMILA stops at a bulletin board with one of
her flyers thumb tacked to it. It's been
vandalized. Overlapping part of her flyer is a
flyer of HARPER, untouched. MARCUS gives
her a moment.)*

MARCUS
Yo J...you okay?

(JAMILA doesn't react.)

MARCUS
J?

JAMILA
Why did I run?

*(HARPER bursts through the doors with her
friends, laughing. She see's Jamila and Marcus
and walks over to them.)*

HARPER

Sorry sis. Those are the breaks. No hard feelings, k?

(JAMILA runs at HARPER with the intention of hitting her, but MARCUS stops JAMILA just in time before she can get to HARPER.)

MARCUS

(Holding JAMILA back.)

Whoa, J! Stop! Don't do this! It's not worth it.

HARPER

Oh my God! Are you crazy?

JAMILA

(Overlapping.)

Whatever Marcus! Go be with her, I don't care!

MARCUS

Wait J...

JAMILA

No Marcus, you wait. I may not be the most popular but at least I'm a decent human being.

(JAMILA storms off in tears.)

HARPER

Can you believe her? She straight up attacked me!

MARCUS

And I would've let her rip you apart if it didn't go on her record for college.

HARPER

Excuse me?

MARCUS

It's messed up, what you did. She didn't deserve that, Harper. If you want to run for president, fine. But then you go out of your way to embarrass her? And completely ruin her chances at the only school she's ever wanted to go to? How sad is your life to have to stoop that low?

HARPER

Jeez Marcus, chill...

MARCUS

How 'bout you grow up?

HARPER

Ok, fine...that's fair.

MARCUS

Nobody treats Jamila that way.

HARPER

Ok, I'm sorry. Can we go back to your place now?

MARCUS

No. We're done Harper. For good.

(MARCUS exits, leaving HARPER alone.)

SCENE 5: JAMILA'S HOME.

(Lights up on JAMILA and NYEMA in their living room. JAMILA is sitting in a chair, staring forward at a mirror as NYEMA studies it.)

NYEMA

It's really not that bad, sis.

JAMILA

Nyema, my Princeton interview is tomorrow and I look crazy.

NYEMA

I tried to tell you about those edges.

JAMILA

I know.

(A beat.)

NYEMA

Let me touch it up.

JAMILA

How? These pieces are hanging on by a thread as it is.

NYEMA

What about a wig?

JAMILA

You know how I feel about wigs. I'm not wearing anything that makes people curious enough to touch it and pull it off. I may as well kiss Princeton goodbye.

NYEMA

It's not over, Jamila.

JAMILA

Maybe this is all a sign from God telling me that no matter what I do, I'll fail at it. Whether I'm interviewing for college or running for Student Body President. I am a complete failure. Maybe Harper was right. Why would I even entertain the thought of Princeton accepting me?

NYEMA

What you think you're missing on top of your head, I guarantee you have more than enough to make up for it inside your head.

JAMILA

Tell that to Princeton.

NYEMA

Maybe I will. I think this is a sign telling you to embrace your roots. Let go and improvise a little bit.

JAMILA

What are you talking about?

NYEMA

I can fix this sis, trust me.

SONG: "YOUR ROOTS"

> LET ME MAKE YOU BEAUTIFUL
> MAKE YOU IN-DEMAND
> MAKE YOU STEP INTO THAT ROOM IN FULL
> COMMAND.

NYEMA (CONT)
MAKE THEM SEE YOUR WORTH.
MAKE THEM SAY YOU'RE IT.
MAKE THEM OFFER A SCHOLARSHIP.

MAKE YOU UNDENIABLE, UNDENIABLE.
UNDENIABLE. THE MOST DESIRABLE.

JAMILA
How?

NYEMA
Easy. Like our ancestors - we work with what we got.

WE'RE MORE THAN SOME STYLE, SOME FAD,
SOME TREND.
WE'RE MORE THAN SOME POPULAR
PHENOMENON
THAT'S COME AND GONE.
FIVE THOUSAND YEARS BEFORE WE WERE
HERE
AND FIVE THOUSAND MORE WHEN WE
DISAPPEAR.
LIKE THE BROWN IN OUR EYES, AND THE
BLACK ON OUR SKIN,
WE ARE BEAUTIFUL WITHIN.
WE COME FROM STRENGTH,
WE COME FROM CULTURE,
WE COME FROM WISDOM AND POWER.
THE CONNECTION WE HOLD
TO OUR ANCESTORS, OUR CREATOR -
SOMETHING UNDOUBTABLY OURS!

THESE ARE OUR ROOTS.
THESE ARE OUR ROOTS.
THESE ARE OUR ROOTS.

NYEMA (CONT)
THESE ARE OUR ROOTS.

YOU COME FROM A LONG LINE OF RESILIENT
AFRICAN WOMEN.
YES, THEY CRIED.
YES, THEY HURT.
BUT THEY NEVER GAVE UP THEIR MISSION.

FIVE THOUSAND YEARS BEFORE WE WERE
HERE
OUR KINGS AND QUEENS RULED WITH NO
FEAR.
LIKE THE SHAPE OF YOUR LIPS AND THE KINKS
IN YOUR FRO,
I HAVE TO MAKE SURE YOU KNOW...

YOU COME FROM STRENGTH,
YOU COME FROM CULTURE,
YOU COME FROM WISDOM AND POWER.
THE CONNECTION YOU HOLD
TO OUR ANCESTORS, OUR CREATOR -
SOMETHING UNDOUBTABLY YOURS!

THESE ARE YOUR ROOTS.
THESE ARE YOUR ROOTS.
THESE ARE YOUR ROOTS.
THESE ARE YOUR ROOTS.

THE ART OF IMPROVISATION
AND ON-THE-SPOT CREATION
IS A SKILL MASTERED BY FEW.
WORKIN' WITH WHAT WE GOT
TO GET JUST WHAT WE WANT:
THIS IS WHAT WE DO.
MAKING MIRACLES HAPPEN,

NYEMA (CONT)
TURNING LEMONS TO LEMONADE:
THIS AIN'T NOTHING NEW.
THIS IS YOUR BLOODLINE.
THIS IS YOUR LINEAGE.
TRUST WHAT'S INSIDE YOU.

NYEMA/JAMILA
WE COME FROM STRENGTH,
WE COME FROM CULTURE,
WE COME FROM WISDOM AND POWER.
THE CONNECTION WE HOLD
TO OUR ANCESTORS, OUR CREATOR -
SOMETHING UNDOUBTABLY OURS!

THESE ARE OUR ROOTS.
THESE ARE OUR ROOTS.
THESE ARE OUR ROOTS.

JAMILA
THESE ARE MY ROOTS.

NYEMA
DON'T LET ANYONE TRICK YOU INTO
BELIEVING
YOU'RE NOT DESERVING OF THE CROWN ON
YOUR HEAD.
DON'T LET ANYONE TRICK YOU INTO
BELIEVING
YOU'RE NOT GOOD ENOUGH. DON'T BE
MISLED.

DON'T LET ANYONE TRICK YOU INTO
BELIEVING

NYEMA (CONT)
YOU'RE NOT WORTHY OF THE GREATNESS YOU
PROCLAIM.
DON'T LET ANYONE TRICK YOU INTO
BELIEVING
YOU'RE NOT BEAUTIFUL, WHEN "BEAUTIFUL"
IS YOUR NAME:

JAMILA. JAMILA. JAMILA.

JAMILA
BEAUTIFUL IS MY NAME.

END SONG.

NYEMA

Go kill that interview.

JAMILA

Thanks, sis.

(Scene shifts back to the school conference room. INTERVIEWER 2 enters.)

INTERVIEWER 2

Jamila Watkins?

JAMILA

Here.

INTERVIEWER 2

You're up!

(JAMILA walks in with the INTERVIEWER. Spotlight on JAMILA.)

INTERVIEWER 2

Hi, Jamila.

JAMILA

Hi.

INTERVIEWER 2

How are you feeling?

JAMILA

I feel...ready.

INTERVIEWER 2

I love that. Well let's jump right in. What makes you ready
for Princeton?

SONG: "ONE OF ONE (FINALE)"

JAMILA
I DONE FELL A THOUSAND TIMES.
TRY'NA FLY WITH BROKEN WINGS.
WITH ALL THE HILLS THAT I HAD TO CLIMB.
I CAN TAKE ON ANYTHING!

I AM FOCUSED.
I AM GROUNDED.
I HAVE CLARITY I NEVER HAD.
I'M READY FOR ACTION.
READY FOR THE WORLD
READY TO TAKE OFF FROM THE LAUNCH PAD.

I AM ONE OF ONE.
AFTER ME, THEY'LL BE NONE TO COME.
I AM ONE OF ONE.
AFTER ME, THEY'LL BE NONE TO COME.
AND I ACCEPT THAT.

JAMILA (CONT)
I WILL ADMIT THAT.
I AM WORTHY OF ALL THE PRAISE.
I WILL RECEIVE THAT.
TRUST AND BELIEVE THAT
ALL OF THE HARD WORK EVENTUALLY PAYS.
I AM ONE OF ONE.
I AM ONE OF ONE.

(Lights down on INTERVIEWER 2. The scene transitions to school the following week.)

I DONE FELL A MILLION TIMES.
BUT I GET UP A MILLION ONE.
CAREFREE, IN MY PRIME.
PLEASE BELIEVE MY WORK AIN'T DONE!

I AM EXCITED.
I AM EAGER.
I AM PREPARED FOR ANY WEATHER.
I AM HOPEFUL.
I AM CERTAIN
A TESTAMENT THAT IT GETS BETTER!

JAMILA/STUDENTS
I AM ONE OF ONE.
AFTER ME, THEY'LL BE NONE TO COME.
I AM ONE OF ONE.
AFTER ME, THEY'LL BE NONE TO COME.
AND I ACCEPT THAT.
I WILL ADMIT THAT
I AM WORTHY OF ALL THE PRAISE.
I WILL RECEIVE THAT.
TRUST AND BELIEVE THAT
ALL OF THE HARD WORK EVENTUALLY PAYS.

STUDENTS

NO MATTER WHAT - I
ALWAYS LOOK UP BE-
CAUSE THERE IS NOTHING
LIKE MYSELF.
I WON'T APOLOGIZE
FOR MY BEAUTY.
FOR MY UNIQUENESS
IS MY WEALTH.

NO MATTER WHAT - I
ALWAYS LOOK UP BE-
CAUSE THERE IS NOTHING
LIKE MYSELF.
I WON'T APOLOGIZE
FOR MY BEAUTY.
FOR MY UNIQUENESS
IS MY WEALTH.

(HARPER enters. JAMILA see's HARPER, but says nothing.)

HARPER

I'm sorry Jamila.

(JAMILA doesn't react.)

HARPER

I was a jerk. For real, for real.

JAMILA

Yeah. You were.

HARPER

Marcus broke up with me.

JAMILA

Yeah, right.

HARPER

He's in love with you. I know he is. The way he came to your defense after I posted the video. He definitely checked me.

JAMILA

Interesting.

HARPER

You guys are super close, but it's more for him. And I couldn't handle it.

JAMILA

I see.

(A beat.)

HARPER

I remember the first time I had a braid fall out.

JAMILA

Really?

HARPER

It was awful. I cried a lot. There's no level of embarrassment that comes close to it. Especially when it happens at school.

JAMILA

Facts.

HARPER

I was wrong for putting you on blast like that.

JAMILA

Apology accepted.

HARPER

YOU ARE GIFTED.
YOU ARE WITTY.
YOU ARE A QUEEN AND A GODDESS.
YOU'RE MY SISTER.
YOU'RE AUTHENTIC.
YOU ARE YOUR ANCESTOR'S GREATEST
SUCCESS!

HARPER/STUDENTS

YOU ARE ONE OF ONE.
AFTER YOU, THEY'LL BE NONE TO COME.
YOU ARE ONE OF ONE.
AFTER YOU, THEY'LL BE NONE TO COME.

(NYEMA enters with an envelope.)

NYEMA

Alright! Moment of truth!

(She hands JAMILA a laptop.)

JAMILA

What's this?

NYEMA

Princeton said they would email you by the end of the day
today, right?

JAMILA

Yeah...

NYEMA

Log-in.

JAMILA

Wow. Okay...okay...no pressure...

>	(STUDENTS gather around JAMILA as she logs
>	into her email account.)

JAMILA

Nothing. No email.

NYEMA

Hit refresh.

JAMILA

Okay.

>	(JAMILA refreshes the page and see's an email
>	from Princeton.)

JAMILA

Oh my God they wrote me.

NYEMA

Girl quit being dramatic and open it already! Princeton's
waiting!

JAMILA

Okay, okay.

>	(JAMILA clicks in the email and slowly reads it.
>	She lets out an audible sigh and cries.)

JAMILA

I got in.

(Everyone erupts with applause.)

NYEMA

Speech!

JAMILA

Thank you everyone. Especially Nyema and especially Marcus.

(MARCUS steps forward.)

JAMILA

Thank you for not giving up on me.

MARCUS

And thank you for not giving up on me.

JAMILA

Wh--

(MARCUS kisses JAMILA.)

MARCUS
(Embarrassed.)
Sorry! I should've asked first!

NYEMA

Nah, you good. She's been waiting on that.

JAMILA

Wow. I guess I would be remiss if I didn't announce my news.

MARCUS

What news?

JAMILA

You and Nyema really showed me what's most important in life. It's why I already decided I'm not going to attend Princeton in the fall.

(Everyone reacts, uncertain.)

NYEMA

Wait, what?

JAMILA

I decided I want to attend a Historically Black College and University. This is why I am going to apply to Howard University!

(Everyone applauds, happy for her decision.)

JAMILA

Of course Princeton would be amazing, but I believe no place can connect me to my roots more than a black college.

NYEMA

Ain't that the truth.

MARCUS

I support it.

JAMILA

Howard is an extremely competitive school to get into, but hopefully they will see what Princeton see's!

NYEMA

A Howard Bison!

MARCUS

We love to see it!

(Everyone cheers.)

FULL COMPANY

NO MATTER WHAT - I
ALWAYS LOOK UP BE-
CAUSE THERE IS NOTHING
LIKE MYSELF.
I WON'T APOLOGIZE
FOR MY BEAUTY.
FOR MY UNIQUENESS
IS MY WEALTH.

NO MATTER WHAT - I
ALWAYS LOOK UP BE-
CAUSE THERE IS NOTHING
LIKE MYSELF.
I WON'T APOLOGIZE
FOR MY BEAUTY
FOR MY UNIQUENESS
IS MY WEALTH.
I AM ONE OF ONE.
AFTER ME, THEY'LL BE NONE TO COME.
I AM ONE OF ONE.
AFTER ME, THEY'LL BE NONE TO COME.
AND I ACCEPT THAT.
I WILL ADMIT THAT
I AM WORTHY OF ALL THE PRAISE.
I WILL RECEIVE THAT.
TRUST AND BELIEVE THAT.
ALL OF THE HARD WORK EVENTUALLY PAYS!

JAMILA	**FULL COMPANY**
I AM ONE OF ONE.	SHE'S UNDENIABLE.
I AM ONE OF ONE.	SHE'S UNDENIABLE.
I AM ONE OF ONE.	SHE'S UNDENIABLE.
I AM ONE OF ONE.	SHE'S UNDENIABLE.

FULL COMPANY

I AM ONE OF ONE!

BLACKOUT.

65